USA TODAY.
CULTURAL MOSAIC

The European American Experience

Karen Sirvaitis

TFCB

Twenty-First Century Books · Minneapolis

> *This book takes a broad look at European Americans. However, like all cultural groups, the European American community is extremely diverse. Each member of the community relates to his or her background and heritage in different ways, and each has had a different experience of what it means to be European American.*

USA TODAY®, its logo, and associated graphics are federally registered trademarks. All rights are reserved. All USA TODAY text, graphics, and photographs are used pursuant to a license and may not be reproduced, distributed, or otherwise used without the express written consent of Gannett Co., Inc.

USA TODAY Snapshots®, graphics, and excerpts from USA TODAY articles quoted on back cover and on pages 14, 16–17, 25, 41, 43, 48, 50–51, 55, 56, 65, and 67
© copyright 2011 by USA TODAY.

Copyright © 2011 by Lerner Publishing Group, Inc.

All rights reserved. International copyright secured. No part of this book may be reproduced, stored in a retrieval system, or transmitted in any form or by any means—electronic, mechanical, photocopying, recording, or otherwise—without the prior written permission of Lerner Publishing Group, Inc., except for the inclusion of brief quotations in an acknowledged review.

Twenty-First Century Books
A division of Lerner Publishing Group, Inc.
241 First Avenue North
Minneapolis, MN 55401 U.S.A.

Website address: www.lernerbooks.com

Library of Congress Cataloging-in-Publication Data

Sirvaitis, Karen, 1961–
   The European American experience / by Karen Sirvaitis.
      p. cm. — (USA TODAY Cultural mosaic)
   Includes bibliographical references and index.
   ISBN 978-0-7613-4088-1 (lib. bdg. : alk. paper)
   1. European Americans—History—Juvenile literature. 2. European Americans—Social life and customs—Juvenile literature. I. Title.
E184.E95S566 2011
973'.0409—dc22   2009045923

Manufactured in the United States of America
1 – DP – 7/15/10

INTRODUCTION:
ACROSS THE ATLANTIC — 5

CHAPTER 1:
LINGO — 8

CHAPTER 2:
ARTS AND ENTERTAINMENT — 20

CHAPTER 3:
SPORTS AND GAMES — 35

CHAPTER 4:
A BELIEF IN FREEDOM — 45

CHAPTER 5:
HONORING THE PAST — 52

CHAPTER 6:
LET'S EAT! — 61

70 FAMOUS EUROPEAN AMERICANS
72 EXPLORE YOUR HERITAGE
74 EUROPEAN AMERICAN SNAPSHOT
75 GLOSSARY
76 SELECTED BIBLIOGRAPHY
77 FURTHER READING AND WEBSITES
78 INDEX

USA TODAY CULTURAL MOSAIC

USA TODAY CULTURAL MOSAIC

INTRODUCTION:
ACROSS THE ATLANTIC

In 1776, when the United States became an independent country, it was home to Native Americans, African Americans, and European Americans. Most of the Europeans were of British descent. People from Britain—the island that contains England, Scotland, and Wales—had been coming to North America in large numbers since the early 1600s. In the early United States, British Americans (also called Anglo-Americans) provided the basis for much of U.S. culture.

Other European Americans, including Dutch, Irish, French, German, Spanish, and Portuguese people, also made their homes in the new United States. They saw the new nation as a place of opportunity and freedom. Many more Europeans wanted to live in the United States. Between 1800 and 1924, more than thirty-five million people left Europe for the United States.

European immigrants came to the United States for different reasons. Many came to escape religious persecution in Europe. Immigrants

Immigrants to the United States *(opposite page and at right)* arrive at Ellis Island in Upper New York Bay in the early 1900s. The immigration station at Ellis Island was built in the 1890s and officially opened in 1892. The station closed permanently in 1954. In 1990 the National Park Service opened the former immigration buildings to the public. Modern visitors go there to learn about the European immigrant experience.

A disease called blight wiped out Ireland's potato crop in the 1840s. About one-third of all Irish families, such as the one at left *(pictured in the* Illustrated London News *in 1848)*, relied on potatoes for their main source of food. Without the food crop, about one million people died of disease or starvation. Another million left Ireland for a better life elsewhere.

also came to escape poverty, unemployment, and hunger in their home countries. For instance, in the late 1840s, about one million Irish people came to the United States to escape famine in Ireland.

Some European immigrants settled in U.S. cities and looked for work. Others became pioneers, heading west to establish farms and ranches. No matter where they settled, most Europeans faced hardships when they arrived in the United States. Some immigrants had a hard time finding jobs and homes. Others found it hard to learn English and adapt to a new culture. Europeans who moved west to the frontier had to struggle against nature. Some Anglo-Americans did not like the new European immigrants and treated them harshly.

While immigrants were glad to be in the United States, many missed their homelands. Over time, European immigrants joined together with those of the same ethnic background. They formed associations for Italian Americans, for instance, and for German Americans. In these communities, European Americans felt comfortable speaking their native languages and following their own traditions. In modern times, many European Americans still retain some European customs.

In the twenty-first century, Europeans continue to move to the United States but in far fewer numbers than before. The new immigrants tend to settle in big cities, which offer education and jobs. The newest European immigrants have formed new ethnic communities, just as earlier immigrants did before them.

Because so many Europeans have moved to the United States, many European customs have become U.S. customs. Let's find out how much of U.S. culture comes from Europe.

CHAPTER 1:
LINGO

British Americans gave the United States one of its most obvious cultural traits—the English language. The language of British settlers, English was also the main language of colonial America and later the new United States. The Declaration of Independence and the U.S. Constitution were written in English. In modern times, English is the main language of the U.S. government, business, and education. Most Americans grow up speaking English. Those who immigrate to the United States usually learn English. The form of English spoken in the United States is called American English.

As a former British colony, the United States adopted English as its official language. The nation's major legal and historic documents, such as the Declaration of Independence (above), are written in English.

MOTHER TONGUES

But English has never been the only European language spoken in the United States. Many early

8 • THE EUROPEAN AMERICAN EXPERIENCE

citizens spoke Dutch, German, Portuguese, or another European language, depending on their country of origin. In the 1800s and early 1900s, European immigrants brought more languages to the United States. These languages included Italian, Russian, Polish, and Greek.

After settling in the United States, many European immigrants continued to speak their native languages with others from their home countries. Some immigrants created foreign-language newspapers. In the early 1900s, European American publishers printed more than twelve hundred newspapers in various European languages. About eight hundred of these papers were in German. Immigrants read the newspapers to keep up with news in their ethnic communities and events in their homelands.

Most European immigrants were also eager to blend in with other Americans. They needed to learn English to succeed in school and in

A Bit about Europe

Europe extends from the Arctic Ocean in the north to the Mediterranean Sea in the south. Its eastern border is the continent of Asia. Its western border is the Atlantic Ocean. Within these borders, Europe holds forty-eight countries.

The people of Europe speak about fifty different languages and more than one hundred dialects, or language variations. Many European languages are similar. They stem from the same roots and use the same alphabets. But some European languages are different from the others. For instance, Russian is written with the Cyrillic alphabet. This alphabet is unlike the Roman alphabet used to write English and most other European languages.

Immigrants learn English at a class for recent newcomers to Cincinnati, Ohio, in 1914. Churches, unions, and charity groups were among a variety of organizations that helped new immigrants adjust to life in the United States.

the workplace. Many European immigrants took English classes or picked up English by trial and error. Immigrants especially wanted their children to learn English so they would succeed in the United States. The children of European immigrants grew up speaking English. They sometimes also learned their parents' native languages at home.

As the children of European immigrants learned English, the number of European-language newspapers in the United States dwindled. In the twenty-first century, only a handful of European-language newspapers remain.

TRACES OF EUROPE

While Europeans learned English, English speakers also learned new words from their European American neighbors. For instance, Italian immigrants used Italian terms such as *ciao* (hello and good-bye), *viva* (long live), and *mamma mia* (literally my momma, but really meaning Oh, my gosh). Soon native English speakers started using these phrases as well. German Americans contributed *kaput* (finished) and hamburger to American English. French speakers gave us *bon voyage* (have a great trip). Jewish immigrants from Russia and other parts of Europe spoke a language called Yiddish. Other Americans picked up some Yiddish words and phrases. One example is *klutz*, which means "a clumsy person."

Yinglish

In the late nineteenth century and early twentieth century, many Jewish Europeans immigrated to the United States. Most came from Russia or the nations of eastern Europe. Most of these immigrants spoke a language called Yiddish. It is a blend of Hebrew (the ancient language of Jews) and many European languages, especially German.

In the United States, Yiddish speakers introduced Yiddish words into English. These include:

- chutzpah: daring or nerve
- glitch: a minor malfunction
- maven: expert
- oy vey: my goodness!
- schlep: to drag or carry something around

The Dutch were early settlers in the United States. Traces of their impact on the English language remain in place-names, such as the Catskill Mountains at left.

European Americans also contributed many place-names to the United States. In colonial times, New York was home to many Dutch immigrants. They named the Catskill Mountains in southeastern New York. *Catskill* means "wildcat creek" in Dutch. A Dutch farmer named the New York City district of Brooklyn after his home village of Breukelen in the Netherlands. Louisiana (named after Louis XIV, a French king) was once home to many French immigrants. They named the Louisiana city Baton Rouge, which means "red stick" in French. They named Lafayette, Louisiana, for the Marquis de Lafayette, a French nobleman. German immigrants named Germantown, Pennsylvania, a neighborhood of Philadelphia. Irish settlers named Dublin, Ohio, after the capital city of Ireland.

ENGLISH WITH A TWIST

In many places in the United States, European Americans blended their native languages with English. Over time, different immigrant groups developed unique dialects. They also developed distinctive accents, or ways of pronouncing certain words.

Many people from the Scandinavian Peninsula (Norway and Sweden) settled in Minnesota. In northern Minnesota, you can hear people speak "Minnewegian." This is English with a slight Scandinavian accent.

People in the Appalachian Mountains of the eastern United States (Appalachia) speak a distinctive English dialect. They use words such as *yonder*, *britches*, and *fetch*. Scholars have traced these words to Scots-Irish immigrants to Appalachia.

The Amish

Germans make up the largest European American group in the United States. Most German Americans no longer speak German. But a religious group named the Amish keeps the German language alive in the United States. The Amish speak a dialect called Swiss German, or Pennsylvania Dutch. In the early 1700s, Amish people came to North America from Switzerland. They first settled in Pennsylvania and later moved to other states. Modern Amish children learn English in school, so they can speak to non-Amish people. At home the Amish mainly speak their unique German dialect.

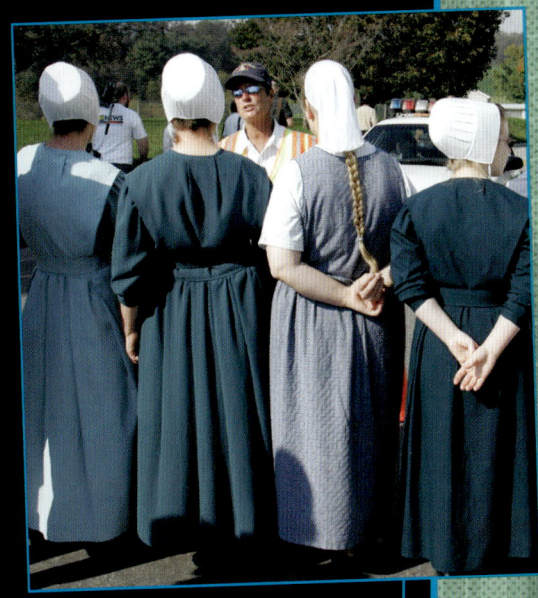

Most Amish women, such as these women in Pennsylvania, wear bonnets and long dresses.

The Cajuns are an ethnic group in Louisiana. Their ancestors were French immigrants to eastern Canada. The Cajuns moved to Louisiana in the late 1700s. They settled around the bayous, or marshes, of rural Louisiana. They had little interaction with people outside their communities and continued to speak French. Over the years, they combined French with English, Native American languages, and African languages learned from African American slaves. They created a new language called Cajun French. In modern times, some Cajuns still speak Cajun French. But most speak English.

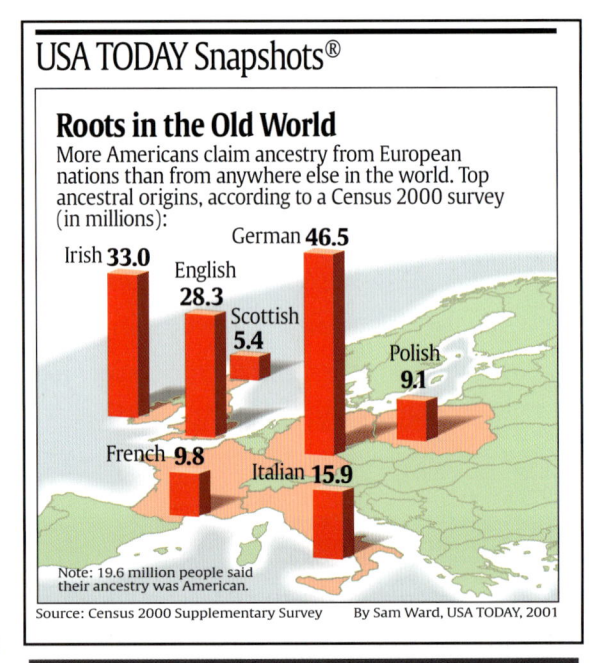

USA TODAY Snapshots®

Roots in the Old World
More Americans claim ancestry from European nations than from anywhere else in the world. Top ancestral origins, according to a Census 2000 survey (in millions):

- German 46.5
- Irish 33.0
- English 28.3
- Italian 15.9
- French 9.8
- Polish 9.1
- Scottish 5.4

Note: 19.6 million people said their ancestry was American.

Source: Census 2000 Supplementary Survey   By Sam Ward, USA TODAY, 2001

Many Americans trace their roots to Europe. This diagram shows the top seven European ancestries in the United States, as of 2001.

THE AMERICAN STORY

Many authors have written about the European American experience. In *Moll Flanders* (1722), British writer Daniel Defoe chronicles Moll's many misfortunes and adventures, including an eight-year stint in the Virginia colony. In the 1820s and 1840s, James Fenimore Cooper wrote the Leatherstocking Tales. The tales consist of five novels set in eighteenth-century America.

No French Allowed

For much of the 1700s, France controlled Louisiana. Many colonists spoke French, while others spoke English or another language. Louisiana became part of the United States in 1803. It became a state in 1812. Most people in the new state spoke English, but some continued to speak French. Many children in Louisiana learned French at home. Many schools taught lessons in French.

In 1921 the Louisiana state government wanted to unite the state's citizens through a common language. It wanted everyone to speak English. The state outlawed French in schools. Teachers punished children who spoke French.

By the 1970s, the state government had a different view of French. It wanted Louisianans to celebrate their French heritage. Schools began teaching French again. Some schools started French immersion programs, where students spoke French all day long. In the twenty-first century, French is again widespread in Louisiana. Colleges teach courses in Louisiana French literature. Publishers sell Louisiana French dictionaries and other books in the language.

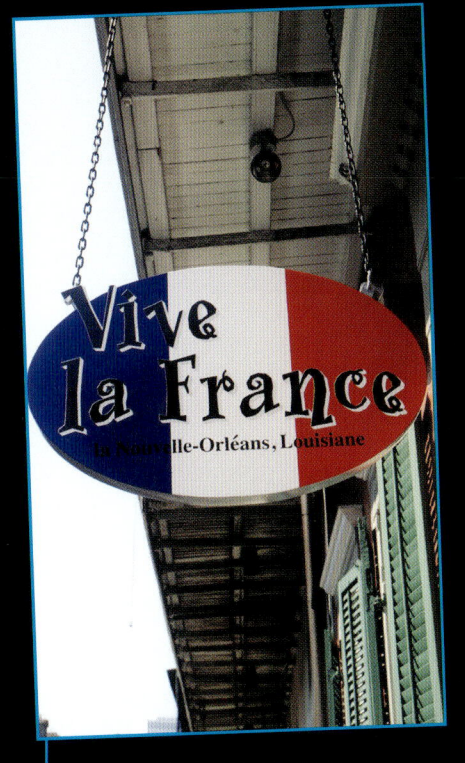

The French Quarter in New Orleans, Louisiana, is the oldest neighborhood in the city.

From the Pages of USA TODAY

Celebrity Accents: It's All Very Tongue-in-Chic

Brit speaks Brit-speak. Maybe it's the latest celebrity lifestyle choice: affecting [faking] a British accent.

Tina Turner and Madonna have been doing it for years; now add... Britney Spears to the list. Two weeks ago, in yet another confrontation with paparazzi [photographers], she suddenly started speaking (screaming, actually) like My Fair Lady's Eliza Doolittle....

Possibly the girl is on to something: Putting on an accent could be a pragmatic [practical] move—as with Democratic presidential candidates Hillary Clinton and Barack Obama, two non-Southerners drawlin' their way through the South on the campaign trail....

Communication experts say some accent changes are normal "linguistic [language] accommodation." Madonna, for instance, started talking like a Brit when she was hanging out with English actor Rupert Everett, and it intensified after she moved to London and married Scottish director Guy Ritchie. Many foreigners who live in the USA for years often lose their accents, at least partly; Bono, for instance, doesn't sound quite as Irish as he did when U2 first appeared in the USA.

"There is nothing unnatural about people making some adjustments in the direction of the locals when they move to a very different accent region," says Jack Chambers, a University of Toronto linguistics professor. "So Madonna, living in England, alters her low vowel in rather so that it comes out as rahther. Most of her accent is middle-class

---

The novels' main character is frontiersman Natty Bumppo, who was born in America. But the stories also include many immigrants from Britain, France, and Germany, as well as many Native Americans.

In *Giants in the Earth* (1927), Norwegian American Ole Rolvaag

16 · THE EUROPEAN AMERICAN EXPERIENCE

Michigander except for these few accommodations...."

But possibly at work here is the mystifying American notion that a British accent connotes [means] more intelligence and culture than a standard American accent....

"Somehow a British accent conveys some sort of higher status," so adopting one can make the insecure feel better, especially performers, [magazine editor Janice] Min says....

Why the inferiority complex? It dates back to Colonial days, when everything from the mother country was esteemed, except for England's aristocrats and anti-democratic class system.

"But people yearn for social hierarchy, England provided the prestige style at the time, and it was World War II that brought (American) self-pride," says Sam Chwat, director of New York Speech Improvement Services, which coaches hundreds of people, including famous actors, on how to acquire or eliminate accents.

Still, aside from PBS [Public Broadcasting Service], Britain's posh tones have not yet invaded American television, though scores of British (and Australian) actors have, while sounding flawlessly American. Hugh Laurie of Fox's *House* is so good at Yank-speak [American English] that many Americans are surprised to hear what he really sounds like on late-night talk shows.

Some foreign-born performers work to banish their accents, while others either can't or don't care: South African-born Charlize Theron watched American TV to bury her Afrikaans accent, but actor-turned-California Gov. Arnold Schwarzenegger still sounds Austrian after decades in the USA.

Putting on the Ritz via an accent can be tricky. English singer Joss Stone, 20, was slammed in the British media for using an American accent at home after making a record in the USA. Even Madonna, whose entire persona is about reinvention and whatever's next, has been mocked back home for her faux [fake] accent. "It's been viewed as treachery, as giving up something she should have been proud of," Chwat says....

As for the continuing value of a British accent: This year's Oscar nominations, announced last week, reinforced the trend of recent years that has British-accented actors as leading contenders for the prize.

—Maria Puente

tells of the life and struggles of Norwegian immigrants in the 1870s. They push westward in covered wagons to farm and settle the North American prairie. Between 1949 and 1959, Swedish author Vilhelm Moberg wrote a series of four books called the Emigrants. The novels were first written in Swedish and later translated into English. They

Willa Cather wrote about many things, including immigrant life on the American frontier.

describe the pains and joys of a family of Swedish immigrants to Minnesota in the mid-1800s. Moberg based some of the characters on his own relatives.

In 1883, at the age of nine, Willa Cather moved with her family from Virginia to Nebraska. At the time, Nebraska was home to large numbers of German and Norwegian immigrants. As a child, Cather knew many immigrants and listened to their stories. As an adult, she wrote about the emotional experiences of immigrants on the frontier, especially the women. Her most famous novels about immigrants are *O Pioneers!* (1913), *Song of the Lark* (1915), and *My Antonia* (1918).

NEW CENTURIES

In the early 1900s, the United States underwent many changes. By then, the West was no longer a wild frontier. Trains and cars had replaced covered wagons. Big cities had grown even bigger. Meanwhile, millions of immigrants arrived in the United States from southern and eastern Europe. Writers began to focus on immigrant life in the cities.

In 1906 author Upton Sinclair published *The Jungle*, a story about the Chicago meatpacking industry. The book describes filthy conditions in slaughterhouses at the turn of the twentieth century. It tells how eastern European immigrant meatpackers endured cruel treatment and dangerous working conditions. Sinclair's work prompted the federal government to pass new food safety laws.

In 1924 the U.S. government cut off most European immigration to the United States. But children of European immigrants continued to write about their immigrant families. Louise DeSalvo was born into an Italian American family in the 1940s. In *Crazy in the Kitchen: Food, Feuds, and Forgiveness in an Italian American Family* (2004), DeSalvo describes generational differences among Italian Americans.

Frank McCourt had a unique immigrant experience. He was born in the United States to Irish immigrant parents in 1930. His family moved back to Ireland when he was a boy. In his acclaimed memoir *Angela's Ashes* (1996), McCourt described his impoverished childhood in Ireland. He later returned to the United States, where he became a teacher and then a writer. He wrote about this immigrant experience in his second book, *'Tis*.

Eamonn Wall is an Irish American poet. He immigrated to the United States in 1982. Wall writes about "the new Irish"—Irish American immigrants of the late twentieth and early twenty-first centuries. Unlike many earlier Irish immigrants, who left Ireland because of famine, the new Irish usually come to the United States for jobs and education.

Gary Shteyngart was born in 1972 in Leningrad (modern Saint Petersburg, Russia). His family emigrated from the Soviet Union (fifteen republics including Russia) to New York when he was seven years old. In *The Russian Debutante's Handbook* (2003), Shteyngart gives Americans a Russian's view of the United States.

Novelist Gary Shteyngart lives in New York and teaches writing at Columbia and Princeton universities.

CHAPTER 2:
ARTS AND ENTERTAINMENT

European Americans brought their musical traditions with them to the United States. For instance, English and Scots-Irish immigrants sang old folk songs and ballads from their home countries. One song, "Botany Bay," told of a robber sent to prison in Australia. In North America, the immigrants changed the song to fit their new surroundings. They changed "Botany Bay" into a folk song called "The Boston Burglar." A later version of the song is called "The Louisville Burglar." Some of the words are the same as in the old "Botany Bay," but the place-names and other details are different.

Klezmorim were traveling Jewish musicians in eastern Europe. They played at weddings and other special events. Their instruments included fiddles, clarinets, and horns. They sang their songs in Yiddish. At the turn of the twentieth century, European Jews brought klezmer music to the United States, where they jazzed it up a little bit.

Klezmer music is a type of secular (nonreligious) music that draws on centuries of Jewish tradition. Klezmer music has many traditional dances too, including waltzes and polkas.

20 · THE EUROPEAN AMERICAN EXPERIENCE

Waylon Thibodeaux was Louisiana's state fiddle champion at the age of sixteen. He is well known for his toe-tapping, high-energy Cajun music.

Klezmer was popular in New York in the 1910s and 1920s but then died out for several decades. In the 1970s, U.S. musicians revived klezmer and started new bands.

The Cajuns also brought folk music with them to Louisiana. Cajun musicians play guitars, fiddles, washboards, and accordions. They sing songs with Cajun French lyrics. Until the mid-twentieth century, Cajun music wasn't well known outside Louisiana. But gradually, more and more Americans learned about it. In the twenty-first century, music lovers can listen to talented Cajun musicians such as fiddler Waylon Thibodeaux. Another popular Cajun group is BeauSoleil (the name means "beautiful sun" in French). In 1997 this band earned a Grammy Award for Best Traditional Folk Album.

FROM ITALY TO AMERICA

Italy has a strong musical tradition. One of the greatest Italian art forms is opera. Started in the fifteenth century, opera combines acting, dance, costumes, instrumental music, and singing. In an opera, the story is told through song. Opera singers have powerful voices that take years to train. For many people, attending an opera is an emotional experience, bringing both tears and laughter.

Enrico Caruso was a worldwide opera sensation. Part of his success came from his many sound recordings (records), which were a cutting-edge technology in the early 1900s. Many of his recordings are still available in the twenty-first century.

Italian immigrant Lorenzo Da Ponte helped introduce opera to the United States. Da Ponte was a librettist, or lyricist, for some of Europe's greatest composers. He started an opera company in New York in 1833. By the mid-1800s, opera houses were springing up across the United States. One of the greatest opera stars of all time was Enrico Caruso. Caruso was Italian, and he always made Italy his home base. But he also lived part-time in New York in the early 1900s. He performed regularly at the Metropolitan Opera in New York City.

In the mid-twentieth century, a host of nightclub singers captivated U.S. audiences. Many of these talents were Italian Americans. They included Frank Sinatra, Dean Martin, and Tony Bennett. The children of Italian immigrants, these singers wanted to blend in with other Americans. Some of them also thought they'd do better in show business if they had American-sounding names. So they changed their names. Dino Crocetti became Dean Martin, for instance, and Anthony Benedetto became Tony Bennett.

22 • THE EUROPEAN AMERICAN EXPERIENCE

Ol' Blue Eyes

Singer and actor Frank Sinatra *(right)* was one of the most famous Italian American entertainers of all time. He was born in Hoboken, New Jersey, to Italian immigrant parents in 1915. He began singing professionally in 1935, at the age of twenty. His career took off when he joined the Tommy Dorsey Orchestra as a singer. His first hit was "I'll Never Smile Again," in 1940. Also in 1940, Sinatra appeared in his first film, *Las Vegas Nights*, along with other members of the Tommy Dorsey Orchestra.

Sinatra left the Dorsey band in 1942 to pursue a solo career. He went on to star in dozens of motion pictures, including *Anchors Aweigh* (1945), *From Here to Eternity* (1953), and *The Manchurian Candidate* (1962). The singer's deep blue eyes earned him the nickname Ol' Blue Eyes.

During World War II (1939–1945), Italy and the United States were enemies. Many Americans feared that Italian Americans were spies or supported Italy in the war. Sinatra's popularity helped relieve some of this fear of Italian Americans. Sinatra also gave Italian Americans a sense of pride.

Throughout his career, Frank Sinatra recorded about fourteen hundred songs. He had thirty-one gold records, which means they sold at least five hundred thousand copies each. Sinatra won ten Grammy Awards, acted in almost sixty films, and won three Academy Awards. He died after a heart attack in 1998.

Italian American pop superstars Lady Gaga *(right)* and Madonna *(far right)* attend a fashion show in New York.

In modern times, the Italian American musical tradition continues with pop singers. The most famous examples are Madonna, whose real name is Madonna Ciccone, and Lady Gaga, who was born Stephani Germanotta. Both singers are descended from Italian immigrants.

HAPPY FEET

Dancing is often a big part of celebrations, such as weddings, festivals, and holidays. European immigrants brought their folk dance traditions with them to the United States.

Polka is a lively dance and musical form. It began in Europe in the mid-1800s. It was popular in Sweden, Poland, Lithuania, Germany, Hungary, Austria, Russia, and Slovenia. Polish immigrants brought their polka tradition with them to the United States. Polka was very popular in the United States in the mid-twentieth century. In the twenty-first century, people still dance the polka at weddings and festivals. Modern polka bands include drums, guitars, tubas, accordions, and clarinets. The basic dance move is a full step followed by two half steps.

February 4, 2008

From the Pages of USA TODAY

With 16 Grammys, Jimmy Sturr Is the Polka Star

Rarely a year goes by that Jimmy Sturr doesn't waltz off with the Grammy for best polka album. He has won 16 trophies in 20 contests and is likely to snatch his 17th this year for *Come Share the Wine*. While Sturr has accumulated as many Grammys as Paul Simon and Sting, he has hardly had their share of the spotlight.

"That's a sore spot with me," the bandleader says of polka's marginalization on a show top-heavy with pop, rock and country stars. "There's no reason a band like ours shouldn't be asked to perform. It's like they pat us on the head and keep moving. I'm not saying we need a whole three minutes, but why not put (polka) and Western swing and Cajun into a medley?" . . .

[Sturr] just finished recording his 119th album. He plays 160 concerts a year nationwide. It's polka 24/7. Even as a teen, rock and pop never lured him.

"I respect heavy metal, but I'm not a fan. I enjoy country because country songs can be adapted to the polka. Everyone here loves polka. We have polka weddings, polka parties, polka radio." . . .

"After winning 16 Grammys, anyone else would be on Letterman or Jay Leno," he says. "I've done something different. I Americanized polka." . . .

"There are hotbeds of polka all over," he says. "It's huge in Texas. I can draw 18,000 people, and 70 percent are 35 and younger. We're like rock stars down there. They go berserk dancing in the aisles."

—Edna Gundersen

Polka music has its roots in central Europe. Musicians in Scandinavia, Great Britain, and Mexico also play versions of the polka. Polka star Jimmy Sturr *(above)* grew up in New York. He has Irish roots.

A group of *klompen* (wooden clog) dancers perform at a festival in Holland, Michigan. The Dutch have a long history of wearing clogs, primarily as work shoes.

Clogging originated in the British Isles. English and Scots-Irish settlers brought the dance with them to the Appalachian Mountains. Early clog dancers wore wooden clogs on their feet, which explains the name. Modern clog dancers wear heavy shoes. They stomp the ground, and the sound of their stomping is part of the performance. In modern times, clogging has spread far beyond the Appalachians. People of all ethnic backgrounds participate in clogging performances and competitions.

Flamenco is a dance form from southern Spain. Dancers wear colorful costumes, clap their hands, drum their heels, and sometimes play castanets. A guitar player accompanies the dancers.

José Greco was a famous flamenco dancer and choreographer.

Italian immigrant José Greco introduced flamenco to millions of Americans. In 1946 he founded the José Greco Dance Company in New York. He also showcased the flamenco style in several Hollywood films. These include *Sombrero* (1953) and *Ship of Fools* (1965). In modern times, several flamenco companies perform in the United States. They include Teatro Flamenco in Santa Fe, New Mexico.

THE SILVER SCREEN

European Americans have been part of the movie business since its beginnings. Charlie Chaplin was born in London, England. He moved to the United States in 1910. Chaplin became famous as a star of silent comic films, including *The Tramp* (1915) and *The Gold Rush* (1925). Swedish immigrant Greta Garbo starred in both silent and talking pictures. Marlene Dietrich began her acting career in Germany and became a Hollywood star in the 1930s. In modern times, European actors continue moving to Hollywood. Modern European American film stars include Catherine Zeta-Jones (born in Wales), Ewan McGregor (born in Scotland), and Antonio Banderas (born in Spain).

Hollywood movies frequently deal with the European American experience. *The Jazz*

Film star Greta Garbo was born Greta Gustafsson in Stockholm, Sweden.

ARTS AND ENTERTAINMENT • 27

Singer (1927) was the first talkie, or movie with sound. It tells the story of a young Jewish American singer. His love of jazz music brings him into conflict with his traditional immigrant parents.

In the 1930s, Hollywood produced many gangster movies. The movies were based on the exploits of real-life gangsters of the 1920s. Many of the real gangsters were Irish American or Italian American. *The Public Enemy* (1931) is a classic gangster film from the 1930s. Its star, James Cagney, was a talented Irish American singer and dancer. But he was most famous for playing tough guys in gangster movies.

The three *Godfather* movies (1972, 1974, and 1990) are the most famous gangster movies of all time. Their creator was Italian American filmmaker Francis Ford Coppola. The movies follow the experiences of several generations of the Corleone family. The Corleones are Italian American gangsters. But the *Godfather* movies are more than just gangster films. They also shed light on the Italian American experience in

The Godfather (the first of three *Godfather* movies) is based on the 1969 novel of the same name, written by Italian American author Mario Puzo. Film legend Marlon Brando *(above, on right)* plays Don Vito Corleone, the title character and the head of the Corleone crime family.

Arnold Schwarzenegger

Austrian American Arnold Schwarzenegger *(left)* is famous as the governor of California and as a leading Hollywood actor. But with his thick Austrian accent, reaching these goals in the United States wasn't easy.

Schwarzenegger is a native of Thal, Austria. He was born in 1947. When he was young, his family made physical fitness a priority. Schwarzenegger became a bodybuilder. He won the Mr. Universe bodybuilding competition in 1967, 1968, and 1969. Over the following years, he earned the title of Mr. Olympia seven times. Mr. Olympia is the highest honor awarded to professional bodybuilders.

In the late 1960s, Schwarzenegger moved to the United States to begin an acting career. His first film was *Hercules in New York* (1970). Schwarzenegger played the role of Hercules, a hero in Greek mythology. But his Austrian accent was very thick. Producers were afraid that audiences wouldn't understand his words. So they used another actor to dub, or record over, his voice. Schwarzenegger got his big break in the 1982 film *Conan the Barbarian*. He followed this with several successful action films, including *The Terminator* (1984) and two sequels. In 2003 and again in 2006, voters elected Schwarzenegger governor of California.

the twentieth century. Some people have criticized the Godfather and other gangster movies for stereotyping Italian Americans. The movies might lead audiences to think that many Italian Americans are gangsters, which is not the case.

ARTS AND ENTERTAINMENT • 29

Nia Vardalos *(right)* was nominated in 2003 for an Academy Award for best original screenplay for her 2002 film *My Big Fat Greek Wedding*, in which she also starred. John Corbett *(left)* plays the non-Greek man she eventually marries.

In the twenty-first century, moviemakers continue to examine the experiences of European immigrants. Greek American Nia Vardalos wrote and starred in *My Big, Fat Greek Wedding* (2002). In this romantic comedy, Vardalos plays Toula Portokalos, a young Greek American woman. She causes a stir in her family by falling in love with a non-Greek young man.

Jim Sheridan and his daughters Naomi and Kirsten Sheridan wrote and directed *In America* (2002). The movie is based loosely on the Sheridans' early struggles in the United States. The story is told through the eyes of the family's elder daughter. Although the Sheridans face unemployment, poverty, and death in their new home, the movie has a hopeful ending. Its message is that people can overcome difficult times.

ART AND ARCHITECTURE

Early on, the United States took its artistic cues from Europe. Aspiring U.S. painters and sculptors went to art schools in Europe. Prominent U.S. architects created buildings based on European styles. For instance, the U.S. Capitol in Washington, D.C., has a neoclassical design. Neoclassicism began in Europe in the mid-1700s. It was based on the stately, geometric forms of public buildings from ancient Greek and Rome.

In the 1920s, art deco was the rage in Paris. This design style features sleek lines and geometric shapes, such as zigzags. American designers loved art deco. They applied it to furniture, household items, and even trains.

U.S. architects created buildings in the art deco style. These include the Chrysler Building and the Empire State Building in New York City. The Miami Beach Art Deco District in Florida has more than one thousand art deco buildings in 1 square mile (2.6 square kilometers).

Art deco began in Paris and soon moved to the United States. The 1930 Chrysler Building showcases art deco design.

ARTS AND ENTERTAINMENT · 31

Thousands of people visited Central Park in New York City to see *The Gates* art exhibit in 2005. Artist Christo, along with his wife, Jeanne-Claude, placed the orange fabric gates along walkways in the park.

Architect Eero Saarinen was a Finnish immigrant to the United States. He created some of the nation's most eye-catching structures. One of them is the Gateway Arch, a giant steel arch on the Mississippi River in Saint Louis, Missouri. Another is the Trans World Airlines Terminal at John F. Kennedy International Airport in New York City. The building resembles a bird taking flight.

The artist Christo Javacheff was born in Bulgaria. He immigrated to the United States in 1964. Known by his single name Christo, he is famous for giant outdoor artworks that interact with the landscape. For instance, in 1983 he encircled eleven islands off the Florida coast with hot pink plastic sheeting. In 2005 he erected seventy-five hundred orange fabric "gates" in Central Park in New York City.

TRENDSETTERS

Europeans have started many fashion trends in the United States. Actress Gina Lollobrigida moved from Italy to the United States in the 1950s. In addition to starring in Hollywood movies, she introduced a

New York Times film critic Bosley Crowther once called popular actress Gina Lollobrigida the Italian doll. Known for her good looks, she was a prominent actress in the 1950s and 1960s. She was also a successful photojournalist.

short and cute hairstyle to U.S. women. Stylists called it the artichoke cut for its resemblance to the spiky vegetable. Not only did U.S. women cut their hair short, but they also dyed it brown to look more like Lollobrigida.

European-born fashion designers have also launched trends in the United States. Oleg Cassini was born in France and grew up in Italy. He designed clothing for First Lady Jacqueline Kennedy in the early 1960s. After Kennedy appeared in Cassini's A-line dresses, jackets with big buttons, and pillbox hats, women across the country imitated her. They began wearing copies of the same styles.

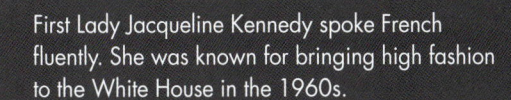

First Lady Jacqueline Kennedy spoke French fluently. She was known for bringing high fashion to the White House in the 1960s.

ARTS AND ENTERTAINMENT • 33

USA TODAY CULTURAL MOSAIC

CHAPTER 3:
SPORTS AND GAMES

The United States is full of gifted athletes in every sport and from every ethnic background. Thousands of European Americans have left their mark in U.S. sports history over the years.

In football, Italian Americans Joe Montana and Dan Marino were champion quarterbacks in the 1980s and 1990s. In the twenty-first century, Irish American quarterback Tom Brady has led the New England Patriots to three Super Bowl victories. Another Super Bowl champ, quarterback Brett Favre, is a French American. Quarterback Jake Delhomme is a Cajun.

In tennis, Italian American Jennifer Capriati and Greek American Pete Sampras took home many trophies in the 1990s. Tennis star Mary Pierce has a French mother and an American father. She lives in the United States but plays for France in team tennis competitions.

In the late twentieth century, Italian-born Mario Andretti dominated U.S. auto racing. Irish American Danica Sue Patrick is also a car racing champion. She is one of the few women to excel in the male-dominated sport.

OPPOSITE PAGE: Carolina Panthers quarterback Jake Delhomme holds the ball in a game in 2009. In 2010 Delhomme signed with the Cleveland Browns.

THIS PAGE: Race car driver Danica Patrick became the first woman to win an Indy car race with her victory in the Indy Japan 300 in 2008.

Mario Andretti

Mario Andretti was one of the most famous and successful race car drivers of all time. He was born in 1940 in northeastern Italy. After World War II, world leaders redrew the boundaries of some European nations. Mario's hometown became part of the former Yugoslavia. The Andrettis didn't want to live in Yugoslavia, which had a repressive government. They applied for visas (legal papers) that would allow them to move to the United States. While waiting for their visas, the family lived in a refugee camp, or temporary settlement, in Lucca, Italy.

Mario Andretti waits to get back on the track while his crew changes tires and refuels his race car at the Indianapolis 500 in 1993.

In 1954 Mario and his twin brother, Aldo, watched the Italian Grand Prix in Monza, Italy. They saw cars drive at more than 100 miles (161 km) per hour along a winding road. The boys became fascinated with car racing.

In 1955 Mario and his family finally arrived in the United States. They came with only $125 in their pockets and spoke no English. The Andrettis settled in Nazareth, Pennsylvania. Their home happened to be close to a racetrack. The fifteen-year-old twins wanted to race cars on that track. They didn't have money to buy a race car, so they built their own.

In his first two seasons of racing, Mario won twenty races. In the 1960s, he went on to win all types of car races. He raced many different kinds of cars on different kinds of tracks. By the time he retired in 1994, Mario had won 111 races, including the Indianapolis 500, the Daytona 500, and the Italian Grand Prix in Monza. Andretti's sons, nephew, and grandson also became race car drivers.

Betsy King is a professional golfer with six major golfing championships and thirty-four Ladies Professional Golf Association Tour victories under her belt.

BOTH SIDES OF THE OCEAN

A number of sports have migrated from Europe to the United States. For example, hockey traces its roots to hurling, an Irish field hockey game. The sport evolved into ice hockey in Canada and then grew popular in the United States. Golf developed in Scotland hundreds of years ago. From there, the sport spread eastward to the rest of Europe and west to the United States. In modern times, golf is one of the most popular U.S. sports. European Americans such as Jack Nicklaus (German American) and Betsy King (Polish American) have become golf champions.

Baseball originated in the 1600s in England, where it was called rounders. In the 1700s, many North American colonists played rounders. Gradually, Americans changed the rules and changed the game's name to baseball. In the twentieth century, many European Americans left their mark on professional baseball. They include Irish American Frank "Tug" McGraw Jr., German American George Herman "Babe" Ruth, Polish American Carl Yastrzemski, and Italian American Joe DiMaggio. In the twenty-first century, Boston Red Sox first baseman Kevin Youkilis descends from Romanian Jewish immigrants.

SPORTS AND GAMES

The Sultan of Swat

The king of all baseball players—nicknamed the Sultan of Swat—was George Herman Ruth, or Babe Ruth *(right)*. Ruth was born in the United States to German immigrant parents. He spoke German fluently as a child. As a boy, George was always getting into trouble, so his parents sent him to boarding school. There, he learned to play baseball.

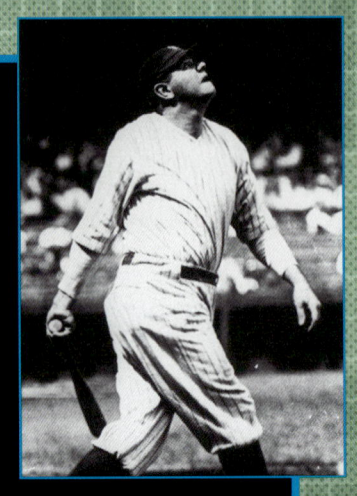

In 1914 Ruth signed with the Boston Red Sox. Because he was only nineteen years old, other players nicknamed him Babe. That same year, World War I (1914–1918) began in Europe. In 1917 the United States joined the war. One of the U.S. enemies was Germany. On the home front, many Americans grew suspicious of German Americans. But most Americans loved Babe Ruth. He helped ease some of the hostility toward German Americans.

In 1919 the Red Sox made what many call the biggest blunder in baseball history. They traded Babe Ruth to the New York Yankees. With the Yankees, Ruth was sensational. He was the first player to hit sixty home runs in one season, a record that held for thirty-four years. His most towering achievement was hitting 714 home runs over his career. It was a record that stood for thirty-nine years. Hank Aaron finally broke it in 1974.

For many years, Americans weren't very interested in soccer. But in the late twentieth century, U.S. children started playing soccer in school. Gradually, the sport became more common in the United States. In modern times, many U.S. soccer players are of European descent. They include Italian American goalkeeper Tony Meola.

Goalie Tony Meola of the Kansas City Wizards prepares to stop the ball during a game against the Colorado Rapids.

He has played on the U.S. National Soccer Team and in Major League Soccer. David Beckham is one of England's most famous soccer players. In 2007 he signed with the Los Angeles Galaxy soccer team and moved to California.

Bicycle racing has long been popular in Europe. But for many years, the sport had few U.S. fans. Two European Americans helped change that. French American Greg LeMond won the Tour de France, Europe's most prestigious bicycle race, three times, in 1986, 1989, and 1990. Lance Armstrong, who has Irish and Scandinavian roots, won the Tour de France a record-breaking seven years in a row, from 1999 to 2005. Armstrong brought a new excitement about bicycle racing to the United States.

Biking champions Lance Armstrong *(left)* and Greg LeMond *(right)* turned Americans into biking fans.

OLYMPIANS

One of the most famous early U.S. Olympic champions was Johnny Weissmuller. Weissmuller was born in Romania to German parents. He and his family moved to the United States in 1905, when Johnny was only seven months old. As a child, he contracted polio, a disease that can cause paralysis. At the advice of his doctor, Johnny began swimming. In the 1920s, he became an Olympic champion. He won five gold medals and one bronze. Weissmuller went on to play Tarzan in a series of twelve motion pictures.

Modern Olympian Tara Lipinski is a Polish American figure skater. In 1997 Lipinski won the U.S. and World Figure Skating Championships. Only fourteen, she was the youngest person to win either title. The following year, she won a gold medal at the 1998 Olympics. She outdid her teammate Michelle Kwan, who had been favored to take the gold.

Olympic champion gymnast Nastia Liukin was born in Moscow, Russia, in 1989. She is the daughter of former Soviet gymnasts Valeri and Anna Liukin. When Nastia was two, her family moved to the United States. Her parents worked as gymnastic coaches. They taught the sport to Nastia. By the age of twelve, she had become an elite gymnast. She was the 2005 and 2007 world champion on the balance beam. In the 2008 Olympics, Nastia earned a gold medal in the all-around competition.

Nastia Liukin has won nine medals in World Gymnastics Championships and five Olympic medals.

40 • THE EUROPEAN AMERICAN EXPERIENCE

TALENT FROM EUROPE

Scouts from professional sports teams often look to Europe for new talent. In fact, professional athletes from Europe are creating a new category of European immigrants in the United States.

Since the 1980s, the National Hockey League (NHL) has recruited hundreds of Europeans to play ice hockey in the United States. Most of the European players are from Russia, the Czech Republic, Finland, Norway, and Sweden. These cold countries are known for producing talented hockey players. Some of the most popular European NHL players are Alex Ovechkin and Pavel Datsyuk from Russia, Kimmo Timonen from Finland, Nicklas Lidstrom and Henrik Zetterberg from Sweden, and Patrik Elias and David Krejci from the Czech Republic.

USA TODAY Snapshots®

Europeans reach 1,000-game milestone

European-born players that have appeared in at least 1,000 regular season games in the NHL:

Player	Country	Games
Jari Kurri	Finland	1,251
Borje Salming	Sweden	1,148
Ulf Samuelsson	Sweden	1,080
Calle Johansson[1]	Sweden	1,050
Teppo Numminen[1]	Finland	1,048
Petr Svoboda	Czechoslovakia	1,028
Fredrik Olausson[1]	Sweden	1,001

1 – active
Note: through Sunday

Source: NHL
By Ellen J. Horrow and Bob Laird, USA TODAY, 2002

Some European hockey players have been in the NHL for many years—racking up more than one thousand games played.

In 2010 Alex Ovechkin was named captain of the Washington Capitals hockey team. He was the first European-born captain in the team's history.

SPORTS AND GAMES

Dirk Nowitzki is the first European-born player in NBA history to receive the NBA Most Valuable Player award, which he won in 2007.

Like the NHL, the National Basketball Association (NBA) began recruiting European players in the 1980s. The NBA has nearly fifty European-born players. They come mostly from Serbia, Croatia, France, Spain, Slovenia, and Lithuania. Born in Croatia in 1968, Toni Kukoc played professional basketball in Europe for six years. In 1990 the Chicago Bulls recruited Kukoc to play in the United States. He became known as the Croatian Sensation. Dirk Nowitzki (German), Linas Kleiza (Lithuanian), Marko Jaric (Serbian), and Sergio Rodriguez (Spanish) are just a few of the many other European NBA players.

April 19, 2006

From the Pages of USA TODAY

Team-First, Back-to-Basics Foreigners Changing NBA

TREVISIO, Italy—Andrea Bargnani is next. Maybe this year. Definitely in 2007.

The 7-foot [2.1 meters] Italian forward with a long-range shooting touch, an inside power game and this town's heart is projected as a top-five NBA draft pick. He will decide by April 29 if he will enter June's draft at age 20 or wait until next year. "I want to be ready," he says.

Bargnani (Barg-NAH-nee) would be the latest in an unprecedented [never-before-seen] foreign invasion of the NBA. International talent comprises a league-record 18 percent of its players. That includes a league-high seven international players on the defending champion San Antonio Spurs, who open the playoffs this weekend looking for their third title in four years, and six on the Phoenix Suns, whose coach made his name in Italy and has used the team-oriented, run-pass-and-shoot game to build the league's fourth-best record this season.

Sixty percent of the NBA's foreign players come from Europe, where they—like Bargnani—are trained from their early teen years in fundamentals-driven basketball factories that produce pinpoint passers, surefire shooters and team-first players.

Perhaps the best: German forward Dirk Nowitzki, the Dallas Mavericks' 7-foot [2.1 m] superstar who is an NBA MVP [Most Valuable Player] candidate again this season.

The European players are just what the coach ordered in an NBA game that has tilted in the past decade toward young talent lacking the fundamentals.

"NBA teams are realizing it's less risky to draft internationals because they're more coachable, more socialized...and have not been Americanized," says former college coach George Raveling, Nike's director of global basketball. Raveling's prediction: International players will comprise 50 percent of the NBA by 2010....

"The Euros and foreign players and coaches," Spurs coach Gregg Popovich says, "are doing things in some ways we have forgotten about and used to do."

—Greg Boeck

USA TODAY CULTURAL MOSAIC

CHAPTER 4:
A BELIEF IN FREEDOM

Many early European colonists in North America came in search of religious freedom. The Puritans were an English religious group, part of the Protestant branch of Christianity. The Puritans broke with the official Church of England in the 1500s. In 1620 a group of Puritans founded Plymouth Colony in Massachusetts so they could practice their religion freely. In 1630 another group of Puritans founded the Massachusetts Bay Colony. The Puritan colonists were strict about their religious practice. They also valued hard work, thrift, and education. They had strong rules about morality, or right and wrong.

Catholicism is another major branch of Christianity. In England in the 1600s, the government sometimes persecuted Catholics. In 1634 English political leader George Calvert established a Catholic settlement in Maryland. Calvert set up his colony as a safe haven for English Catholics.

In 1682 Englishman William Penn established the colony of Pennsylvania. Penn was a Quaker, or

OPPOSITE PAGE: People mill about the entrance to Saint Patrick's Cathedral in New York City. Many Catholics came to America to escape persecution, but they faced prejudice in their new homeland as well.

THIS PAGE: Quaker William Penn, the founder of the colony of Pennsylvania, was a strong believer in democracy and religious freedom.

member of the Religious Society of Friends. This group shares some beliefs with Christianity. But it is an independent religion that places importance on peace and human welfare. Like Puritans and Catholics, Quakers often suffered persecution in England. The new Pennsylvania Colony protected the religious freedom of all citizens, not just Quakers. The colony of Rhode Island, established in 1636, also offered religious freedom to all colonists.

After the United States became a nation, it guaranteed religious freedom to citizens. The First Amendment of the U.S. Constitution says that people from any religious background can safely practice their faith in the United States. After the nation's founding, millions more Europeans came to the United States seeking religious freedom.

In the twenty-first century, European Americans practice a variety of religions. Many are Christians and belong to either the Protestant or the Roman Catholic branch of Christianity. Some belong to the Eastern Orthodox branch of Christianity. Other European Americans are Jewish. Others practice Islam. European religious traditions are the center of family life for many European Americans. Other European Americans no longer practice the religions of their immigrant ancestors.

EUROPEAN AMERICAN CHRISTIANS

Protestants make up the largest religious group in the United States. Among European Americans, most people of German descent are Protestants. Norwegian, Swedish, and British Americans are also mostly Protestants. Protestantism includes many separate groups, such as Baptists, Lutherans, and Episcopalians. The Amish practice their own distinctive form of Protestantism.

European Muslims in the United States

Muslims are people who practice the Islamic religion. This faith began on the Arabian Peninsula in the A.D. 600s. In the following centuries, the religion gained many followers. The Ottoman Empire, based in Turkey, conquered parts of eastern Europe in the 1300s. The Ottomans introduced Islam to the region. Some Europeans adopted the faith, while most others practiced Christianity.

Early European immigrants to the United States included a small number of European Muslims, mostly from eastern Europe. Muslims from Poland, Russia, and Lithuania started the American Mohammedan (Islamic) Society in New York City in 1907. Meanwhile, Muslims from the Middle East and North Africa also moved to the United States.

Back in eastern Europe, Muslims often fought with their Christian neighbors. The fighting was particularly fierce on the Balkan Peninsula in southeastern Europe. In a series of wars in the 1990s, militias in the Balkan states attacked and slaughtered Muslims. To escape the violence, many European Muslims moved to the United States. In the twenty-first century, Chicago, Illinois, and Saint Louis, Missouri, have sizable communities of Muslim immigrants from southeastern Europe.

European Muslims protest outside United Nations headquarters in New York City. They opposed UN policies enacted during a war in the Balkans in the 1990s.

A BELIEF IN FREEDOM · 47

Catholics make up about 24 percent of the U.S. population. Many Americans of Irish, Italian, Polish, French, Spanish, and Lithuanian descent are Catholic. Some German Americans are also Catholics.

Irish Americans have had a big influence on Catholicism in the United States. Most Irish immigrants arrived in the late 1840s, during the Great Irish Famine. After reaching the United States, many Irish men took jobs as laborers on canals, railroads, and other construction projects. Many female Irish immigrants took jobs as nannies and servants in the homes of wealthy Anglo-Americans. The Irish immigrants were very religious. Many gave large portions of their meager earnings to the Catholic Church. In New York City, Irish immigrants built the grand Saint Patrick's Cathedral on Fifth Avenue. The money to build the church came mostly from poor immigrant workers. Catholic churches soon became the center of Irish immigrant life.

In the 1800s and early 1900s, more than four million Italian immigrants arrived in the United States. Most of them were Catholic. They were not welcome in Irish American Catholic churches, so they

USA TODAY Snapshots

Irish plentiful in America

The number of U.S. residents that claim Irish ancestry is almost 9 times the population of the Republic of Ireland.

(in millions)

U.S. residents with Irish ancestry: 34.3

Ireland's population 3.9

Source: U.S. Census Bureau

By Robert W. Ahrens, USA TODAY, 2004

More than one million Irish people came to the United States to escape the Great Famine (1845–1849). Their descendants in the United States far outnumber the population of the modern Republic of Ireland.

built their own. Italian Americans continued the traditions of their ancestors in Italy. For instance, they celebrated *festas*, or feast days. These holidays honor Catholic saints, or holy people.

Some European Americans adhere to the Eastern Orthodox religion. The Eastern Orthodox Church split from the Roman Catholic Church in A.D. 1054. Eastern Orthodox churches are common in Greece, Russia, and eastern Europe. In the United States, about three million Americans of Russian, Bulgarian, Serbian, and Greek descent follow an Eastern Orthodox religion. Most Eastern Orthodox families pray before icons, or images of saints. In many U.S. cities, Eastern Orthodox immigrants have built ornate churches. Worship services there include many elaborate rituals. The clergy chants, or sings in simple tones. Worshippers chant in response.

EUROPEAN AMERICAN JEWS

After the Jewish state of Israel, the United States is home to the second-largest Jewish population in the world. About 2 percent of the U.S. population practices Judaism. Most Jewish Americans trace their roots to Europe.

Most European Jewish immigrants arrived in the United States in the late 1800s and early 1900s. At first these immigrants lived in poverty in big cities such as New York. The younger generation of European Jewish immigrants quickly became Americanized. They learned English and

This synagogue, or temple, is in the southern state of Georgia. Synagogues are Jewish houses of worship. Most American Jews trace their roots to eastern and central Europe.

From the Pages of USA TODAY

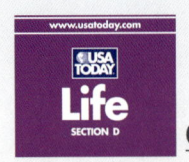

October 30, 2006

Where Religious Freedom Rings; the Baltimore Basilica Stands as a Pillar to the First Amendment and Its Guarantees

New York's St. Patrick's Cathedral might be the most famous Catholic church in America, but Baltimore's old cathedral—the Basilica of the National Shrine of the Assumption of the Blessed Virgin Mary, to use its proper name—is indisputably the most historic. Now, after a two-and-a-half-year, $32 million restoration, all Americans beginning on Saturday can discover this marvel of federal period architecture as its designers intended: an architectural expression of the American commitment to religious freedom, the first of human rights....

We can thank two 19th-century men of genius for the Baltimore Basilica's classic proportions and luminous interior. One, Archbishop John Carroll, was the first Roman Catholic bishop of the newborn USA; the other, Benjamin Henry Latrobe, was the foremost American architect of the day, a friend of Thomas Jefferson, and the first architect of the U.S. Capitol.

John Carroll... wanted the country's first cathedral to speak in a distinctively American architectural idiom and to embody the Catholic commitment to the First Amendment's guarantee of religious freedom.

So Carroll turned to Latrobe, the son of a Moravian [Czech] pastor, and Latrobe (who likely consulted Jefferson)

---

opened businesses. Some attended college. After being educated, many Jewish immigrants moved out of poverty into good-paying jobs.

But Jewish immigrants faced discrimination from other Americans. Some companies wouldn't hire Jews. Some colleges wouldn't admit Jewish students. Jews across the United States stuck together. They mostly lived in all-Jewish neighborhoods. They built produced an American adaptation of classical design that deployed diffused light to express the freedom the human spirit must enjoy in its response to God. The result was a cathedral church whose stateliness and luminosity express a profound respect for what Pope John Paul II, who prayed in the Baltimore Basilica in October 1995, called "the sanctuary of conscience." . . .

A fascinating document touching a long forgotten part of the Baltimore Basilica's past recently came to light at nearby Fort McHenry, whose bombardment during the War of 1812 caused Francis Scott Key to write the "Star Spangled Banner." Had Fort McHenry fallen, the walls of the basilica, which rests on the highest hill in downtown Baltimore, were to be manned as the last line of defense against the British army. It seems, somehow, appropriate, because Baltimore's old cathedral has always been an important part of a line of defense: the defense of religious freedom.

Now, in an age when religious freedom is under threat, not from atheistic ideologies but from irrational violence in the name of God, the restored Baltimore Basilica is more than a stunningly beautiful building—although it is surely that. It also invites every visitor to be a defender of the "sanctuary of conscience" in which humanity carries on its conversation with God.

—George Weigel

Baltimore Basilica in Baltimore, Maryland, is a historic Catholic church. It was built in the early 1800s.

synagogues, Hebrew schools, and Jewish community centers.

In the twenty-first century, many Jewish Americans no longer live in Jewish neighborhoods. Some have married non-Jews. But the Jewish community in the United States is still strong. Many Jews carry on the religious traditions of their European immigrant ancestors.

A BELIEF IN FREEDOM • 51

CHAPTER 5:
HONORING THE PAST

When Europeans came to North America, they brought their traditional holidays and celebrations with them. European immigrants also established new holidays in the United States. Some holidays have meaning for only a particular ethnic group or religion. But many ethnic celebrations have become important days for all Americans.

A family opens gifts on Christmas Day. Christmas is a major holiday for Christians, although some non-Christians in the United States also mark the day as a holiday.

RELIGIOUS HOLIDAYS

In the United States, most people of European ancestry are Christians. Some of the nation's biggest holidays are Christian holidays, namely Christmas and Easter. During these holidays, most Americans get time off from work or school, no matter what their religion.

Christmas honors the birth of Jesus, an ancient religious leader. His life and teachings are the basis for Christianity. People observe the holiday by giving one another presents, decorating their homes with colored lights, and eating with friends and family. Many Christians also attend church on Christmas.

Easter celebrates the death and resurrection (rebirth) of Jesus. The holiday always falls on a Sunday in March or April, depending on the cycle of the moon. Many Christian families celebrate Easter by attending church. They also eat a large meal with relatives. Some families dye Easter eggs. Children also hunt for Easter eggs hidden around the house. Ukrainian Americans brought the art of making *pysanky*, or elaborately decorated Easter eggs, to the United States.

Many Catholic Italian Americans honor saints by holding feast days. The Feast of San Gennaro, for instance, honors the patron saint (protector) of Naples, Italy. In Little Italy—a historically Italian

Christmas Crackdown

Christmas in North America wasn't always a festive occasion. In Massachusetts the Puritan colonists thought it was ungodly to celebrate at Christmastime. They thought people should observe the holy day only with religious worship. From 1659 to 1681, it was against the law to celebrate Christmas in Boston.

But other non-Puritan Americans wanted to celebrate Christmas. In 1819 and 1820, British American author Washington Irving wrote a group of short stories and essays called *The Sketch Book of Geoffrey Crayon, Gent*. Some stories told of warm, loving, and peaceful Christmas celebrations in an English home. They talked of Saint Nicholas (Santa Claus) riding into town on a horse. Irving's stories encouraged Americans to celebrate Christmas with more gusto. In 1870 Christmas became an official U.S. holiday.

American neighborhood in New York City—celebrants parade a statue of Gennaro through the community every day for nine days. Then they place the statue on a church altar. Afterward, people hold a large celebration with Italian music and food.

European American Jews celebrate many religious holidays. Rosh Hashanah is the Jewish New Year. It usually falls in September. Yom Kippur is the most sacred Jewish holiday. It is the Day of Atonement—a day to ask for God's forgiveness for one's sins. The holiday takes place ten days after Rosh Hashanah. Jews celebrate Passover for eight days in spring. This holiday commemorates the Exodus, when Jews escaped from slavery in ancient Egypt. During Passover, Jews eat one or two large feasts called Seders. During the Seders, they retell the story of the Exodus.

A Jewish family reads the biblical story of the Exodus during a Seder meal. The meal includes a variety of symbolic foods, wine, and an unleavened crackerlike bread called *matzo*.

Every year, European American Muslims observe the holy month of Ramadan. Ramadan is the ninth month of the Islamic calendar. It falls at a different time each year. During Ramadan Muslims do not eat between sunrise and sunset. Ramadan ends with a three-day festival called Eid al-Fitr. During this festival, families gather to eat, dance, and exchange gifts.

HOLIDAY TRANSPLANTS

Observant Christians fast (abstain from certain foods) and pray for forty days leading up to Easter. This period is called Lent. It begins on a Wednesday, called Ash Wednesday. On the day before Ash Wednesday, Shrove Tuesday, people often celebrate before starting the fast. In France the celebration is called Mardi Gras, which means "Fat Tuesday." French Catholic settlers brought the Mardi Gras tradition with them to New Orleans in the early 1700s. In modern times, New Orleans' Mardi Gras celebration is world famous. It features colorful parades with big floats and people dressed in wild costumes. People from all religious backgrounds travel to New Orleans to join the party.

USA TODAY Snapshots®

Tone down the party?
What people think New Orleans should do about Mardi Gras this year:

- Scale back **39%**
- Celebrate like always **33%**
- Don't celebrate at all **22%**
- No opinion **6%**

Source: USA TODAY/CNN/Gallup Poll of 1,006 adults Jan. 20-22. Margin of sampling error: ±3 percentage points.

By Karl Gelles, USA TODAY, 2006

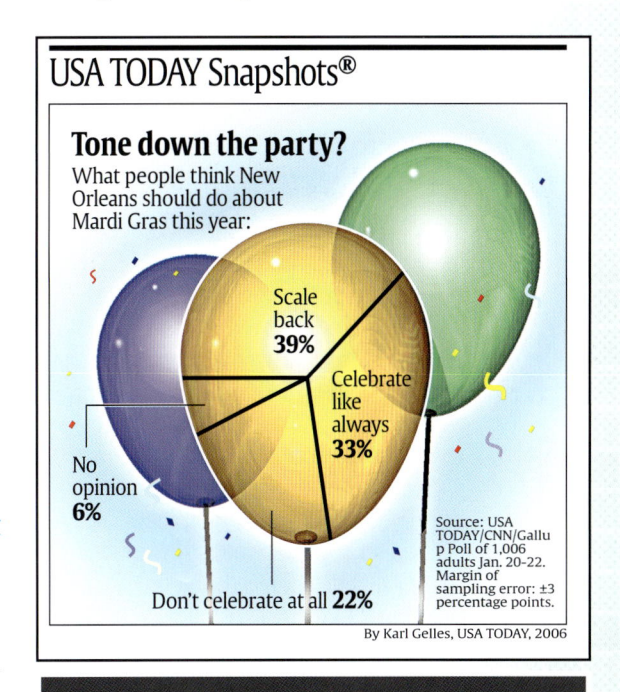

Mardi Gras is a raucous party in New Orleans. But after Hurricane Katrina hit the city in 2005, some people wanted to scale back the celebration.

HONORING THE PAST

February 22, 2009

From the Pages of USA TODAY
Mardi Gras Keeps Marching On

NEW ORLEANS—It's hard to feel the country's economic pinch inside the cavernous holding den of Krewe of Muses, the all-female Mardi Gras parade group.

A day before their parade, women pushed shopping carts full of plastic beads and loaded oversize, elaborately spray-painted floats—26 feet [8 m] in all—with stuffed animals, felt spears, toy footballs and hand-glittered shoes—more than $1 million worth of glitzy attraction.

Outside, one of the most withering economic recessions in U.S. history grips the country. In New Orleans, it's Mardi Gras, an event unmoved by recessions, depressions or catastrophic floods. This year, only three of the 49 Mardi Gras parades in the greater New Orleans area have been canceled. The show goes on.

"The worse the economy gets, the more successful Mardi Gras is," says Staci Rosenberg, a real estate attorney and Muses captain. "People view it as such a critical part of their mental health, such an integral part of their tradition. They won't let it go easily."

Only widespread disease or war has ever stopped the famed, citywide revelry. Since the parades began in 1857, New Orleans Mardi Gras has been entirely canceled only 13 times—including for a yellow fever epidemic, the Civil War and each world war—says Arthur Hardy, a Mardi Gras historian and guide publisher. The last full cancellation: 1945, the last year of World War II. . . .

In 2006, with much of the city still in mud-caked ruin from Hurricane Katrina, Mardi Gras rolled through the drier parts of the city. . . .

[Says Hardy,] "It's genetically encoded into our DNA. It's who we are."

—*Rick Jervis*

The 2010 Mardi Gras celebration (above) in New Orleans was one of the biggest since the 1990s.

The Blessing of the Fleet is a southern European tradition. It began in fishing communities along the Mediterranean Sea. In port cities, the local priest prayed over each fishing vessel. He asked God to protect the fishers and provide them with a season of bountiful harvests. European Catholic immigrants brought the tradition with them to the United States. In many seaside cities along the Atlantic, Gulf of Mexico, and Pacific coasts, modern European Americans bless the fleet at the start of each fishing season. They decorate their boats and parade them through the harbor. A priest blesses each vessel, one by one. On board, friends and family eat and drink to celebrate the beginning of the fishing season. In some communities, the Blessing of the Fleet is a weekend celebration. Thousands of people celebrate by eating fresh seafood and listening to live music.

Saint Patrick's Day takes place every year on March 17. The holiday came to the United States with the Irish. It honors a missionary, or religious teacher, named Patrick. He brought

Crowds gather to see the Chicago River turn green as part of Chicago's yearly celebration of Saint Patrick's Day. Irish immigrants came to the city in large numbers in the 1800s and found jobs as meatpackers, police officers, maids, and construction workers.

Christianity to Ireland about A.D. 400. Irish soldiers serving in the British army organized the first Saint Patrick's Day parade in North America. It took place in New York in 1762. Since then Irish Americans have added to the celebration. They honor Irish culture with food, music, and parades. New York City's Saint Patrick's Day parade is the largest parade in the world. Nearly 150,000 people participate in the event. Three million others line the streets to watch the five-hour-long show. The color green symbolizes Ireland. To honor Saint Patrick's Day in Chicago, the city uses vegetable dye to turn the Chicago River green. Huge Saint Patrick's Day parades are also held in Boston, Massachusetts; Philadelphia, Pennsylvania; and Savannah, Georgia. Lots of people who aren't Irish join in the fun.

Oktoberfest first took place in Munich, Germany, in 1810. The sixteen-day fall festival originally celebrated a royal marriage. By 1960 Oktoberfest had turned into a worldwide celebration. In the United States, German Americans hold Oktoberfest in many towns. The largest Oktoberfest is held in Cincinnati, Ohio, where many German Americans live. Some festival participants dress in nineteenth-century German clothing. Traditional German food, music, beverages, and dancing create a lively atmosphere.

U.S. HOLIDAYS

Several official U.S. holidays honor the achievements of Europeans in America. In 1492 Italian navigator Christopher Columbus sailed to the Americas. At the time, Europeans did not know the Americas existed. After the founding of the United States, European Americans looked to Columbus as a hero.

In the mid-1800s, Italian American immigrants sometimes suffered discrimination in the United States. They wanted other

Fireworks cap Fourth of July celebrations across the United States each year.

Americans to know that the national hero Columbus was Italian. Italians pushed the U.S. government to create a Columbus Day celebration. President Franklin D. Roosevelt made Columbus Day a federal holiday in 1934. The holiday falls on October 12, the day Columbus first made landfall in the Americas, but is celebrated on the second Monday in October.

In 1775 Americans began the Revolutionary War (1775–1783) to win independence from Great Britain. On July 4, 1776, U.S. founders signed the Declaration of Independence. It officially stated that the American colonies were free of British rule. John Hancock, of British descent, was the first lawmaker to sign the document. One year later, on July 4, 1777, Americans celebrated the first Independence Day to show their commitment to independence. They finally won the war for independence in 1783. By the early 1800s, Independence Day had grown in importance. People celebrated with parades, picnics, and fireworks. In the twenty-first century, Americans celebrate Independence Day to honor the birth of the United States.

USA TODAY
CULTURAL MOSAIC

CHAPTER 6:

LET'S EAT!

Throughout the United States, almost every household serves at least some European-based entrées, side dishes, and desserts. Ethnic restaurants also offer Americans a taste of authentic European cooking. From mustard (Romanian) to hot dogs (German) to ice cream (Italian), European foods have become a regular part of the U.S. diet.

Each ethnic group that comes to the United States brings with it flavorful recipes. Immigrants from southern Europe, including Italy, Portugal, Spain, and Greece, have introduced other Americans to the Mediterranean diet. Mediterranean dishes include lots of olive oil, lemons, fresh herbs such as basil and oregano, fresh vegetables, garlic, and small amounts of fish and meat.

The French introduced haute cuisine to the U.S. diet. *Haute cuisine* means "high cooking," which is another name for fancy food. Haute cuisine features rich sauces and elaborate dishes that can take hours or even days to prepare. Baguettes (long, thin, crusty loafs of bread), omelets, quiche, and café au lait (coffee with hot milk) also came to the United States from France.

Immigrants to the United States brought a rich variety of foods with them. For example, Italians brought pizza and pasta *(opposite page)*. French immigrants brought a long loaf of bread known as the baguette *(right)*. These foods have become American staples.

LET'S EAT! • 61

ON THE MENU

After arriving in the United States, some European immigrants opened restaurants. Some immigrant-run restaurants served standard American food, such as meat loaf and mashed potatoes. Others dished out recipes from the owners' homelands.

At first, ethnic restaurants were usually located in the ethnic neighborhoods of large cities. You'd find Italian restaurants in Italian neighborhoods and Greek restaurants in Greek neighborhoods. The customers were other immigrants. But the doors were also open to nonimmigrants. Before long, non-European Americans came to learn about all sorts of new flavors and dishes.

Over the years, Americans came to love pizza, which arrived with Italian immigrants. Americans learned about the Swedish smorgasbord, a buffet offering hot and cold meats, smoked and pickled fish, cheeses, salads, and relishes. Americans ate corned beef sandwiches and lox and bagels in Jewish delis. Grocery stores began to stock olive oil, pasta, and Parmesan cheese so that

This Jewish deli in New Jersey serves foods such as pastrami sandwiches, bagels, smoked fish, matzo ball soup *(front)*, and latkes (potato pancakes, behind the soup).

62 · THE EUROPEAN AMERICAN EXPERIENCE

Potato Soup

The German name for potato soup is *kartoffelsuppe*. It is perfect for a light evening meal. To make a vegetarian version, leave out the pork and use water instead of chicken broth.

INGREDIENTS
6 medium potatoes, peeled and cubed
2 medium carrots, peeled and chopped
2 stalks celery, chopped
1 large onion, peeled and chopped
1 ham bone, or 1 smoked pork hock
6 cups chicken broth or water
1 teaspoon salt
½ teaspoon pepper

1. Place all ingredients in a large kettle, and bring to a boil over high heat.
2. Reduce heat to low, cover, and simmer 20 to 30 minutes, or until vegetables are tender.
3. Remove ham bone with a spoon. Mash vegetables into the broth with a potato masher.
4. Stir well and serve.

Serves 4 to 6

customers could make their own Italian dishes at home. In modern times, supermarkets stock the ingredients for almost every kind of European-style dish, from Bavarian cream pie to Irish stew.

FOOD CRAZES

At different times, European foods have exploded in popularity in the United States. In the 1960s, for instance, French cooking was all the rage. Julia Child helped start the trend. Child was born in California but studied French cooking in Paris. She wrote a book called *Mastering the Art of French Cooking* (1961) and hosted a television show called *The French Chef* (1963–1972). On this show, Child showed U.S. homemakers how to prepare sophisticated dishes such as bouillabaisse à la Marseillaise (a fish stew). French cooking got another boost in 2009 with the movie *Julie & Julia*. The film is based on Child's career and a modern-day New Yorker who tried to master all her recipes.

In the 1960s and 1970s, U.S. cooks went crazy for fondue, a Swiss dish. The word *fondue* comes from the French word for "melt." Cheese fondue consists of a pot of melted cheese and other ingredients. People dip crusty bread into the cheese.

This fondue features nut bread and vegetables, which diners will dip into the pot of melted cheese.

64 • THE EUROPEAN AMERICAN EXPERIENCE

August 13, 2009

From the Pages of USA TODAY

Julia Child Film Fires up Interest in French Cuisine, Old TV Show

NEW YORK—*Voila!* Marketers are tapping into the buzz of interest in classic French cuisine, thanks to the popularity of the movie *Julie & Julia*.

The movie, written and directed by Nora Ephron, combines the memoirs of famed chef Julia Child and young fan Julie Powell.

Since opening at No. 2 at the box office last weekend behind *G.I. Joe*, the movie has spurred sales of Powell's book on a year of cooking all the recipes in Child's landmark *Mastering the Art of French Cooking*, and even higher sales of the 48-year-old cookbook.

But the movie has also been a boost for restaurants and for the Public Broadcasting Service.

Child, who died in 2004 at age 91, was the star of *The French Chef*, which aired on PBS for more than 10 years, and other shows.

PBS has up to 1,000 hours of Child video on its website, and its top 10 video streams are all Child....

A $35 Child menu special, introduced Tuesday by the Culinary Institute of America at its Escoffier Restaurant in Hyde Park, N.Y., drew nearly 400 reservations, vs. a typical 150 in August....

"It was a natural for the college to celebrate her legacy," says Stephen Hengst, a Culinary Institute spokesman. "We had a number of people inquiring about recipes that were made in the film."

—Theresa Howard

Julia Child was a popular cook and TV personality. She brought French cooking to American kitchens through her cookbooks and her televised cooking shows.

Skewered Lamb

Skewered lamb is especially good when cooked the Greek way — on an outdoor grill — but is also delicious when broiled in the oven. You can vary this recipe by alternating pieces of marinated meat (beef or chicken work as well) with chunks of green pepper, onion, and tomato. Ask an adult for help with the broiling or grilling.

INGREDIENTS

- 2 tablespoons olive oil
- 3 tablespoons lemon juice
- ½ teaspoon salt
- ⅛ teaspoon pepper
- ½ teaspoon marjoram
- 2 pounds lamb, cut into 2-inch cubes
- 1 lemon, cut into wedges

1. Mix all the ingredients except lamb and lemons in a large, flat dish.
2. Add lamb and stir to coat pieces well. Cover the dish with plastic wrap, and let stand in the refrigerator for at least 30 minutes.
3. Spear the cubes of meat onto 4 long metal skewers. Place skewers in a shallow broiling pan.
4. Place the oven rack about 6 inches from the top of the heat source. Turn on the oven to broil.
5. Broil meat for 10 minutes. Then turn over skewers, and broil for 10 minutes more.
6. Holding skewers with a pot holder, remove lamb with a fork and serve with lemon wedges.

Serves 4

When the fondue craze hit, Americans threw fondue parties. Kitchen stores sold special fondue pots, plates, and forks. Chefs also served fondue variations, such as chocolate fondue for dessert.

The Mediterranean diet, with its emphasis on fresh herbs, vegetables, and olive oil, came into vogue in the United States in the 1990s. Doctors say that the Mediterranean diet is one of the healthiest in the world.

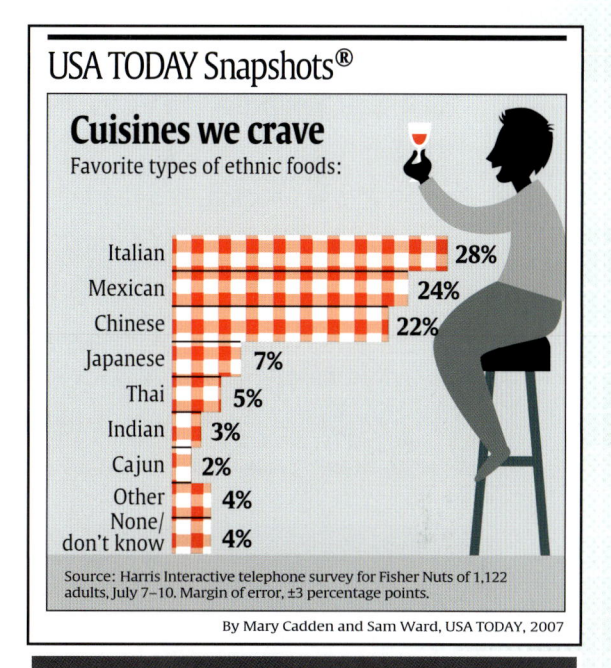

USA TODAY Snapshots®

Cuisines we crave
Favorite types of ethnic foods:

Cuisine	Percentage
Italian	28%
Mexican	24%
Chinese	22%
Japanese	7%
Thai	5%
Indian	3%
Cajun	2%
Other	4%
None/don't know	4%

Source: Harris Interactive telephone survey for Fisher Nuts of 1,122 adults, July 7–10. Margin of error, ±3 percentage points.

By Mary Cadden and Sam Ward, USA TODAY, 2007

Italian food tops the charts of favorite ethnic foods in the United States.

REGIONAL COOKING

In many regions of the United States, ethnic food traditions live on. For instance, throughout the Midwest, many restaurants serve authentic, old-fashioned German cuisine. Sauerbraten (marinated pot roast), sauerkraut (brined cabbage), and spaetzle (small dumplings) are almost always on the menu.

Pasty shops are common in the Upper Peninsula of Michigan. A pasty is a dough pie, usually filled with any combination of ground beef, potatoes, vegetables, and cheese. The pasty originated in the mining communities of Cornwall, England. Instead of stopping work to eat a full meal, miners could eat pasties on the job. In the 1800s, Cornish immigrants brought the tradition with them to the mines of

LET'S EAT! • 67

northern Michigan. Many immigrant families opened pasty shops. In the Upper Peninsula, the mines are mostly closed, but pasty shops are still common.

In Minnesota some restaurants specialize in foods brought to the state by Scandinavian immigrants. These dishes include Swedish pancakes, lingonberry preserves, baked cod, and *lefsa*, or Norwegian potato flatbread. Polish, Italian, Greek, Russian, and French restaurants are common in many large U.S. cities. Detroit's Greektown, for instance, has a host of Greek restaurants.

Wolfgang Puck

Wolfgang Puck *(right)*, a celebrity chef, was born in Austria in 1949. As a child, he learned to cook from his mother, who worked as a pastry chef. He also trained under several chefs in France before moving to the United States in 1973. He immediately found work as a chef. A few years later, he opened his own restaurant in Los Angeles.

Although he's Austrian, Puck favors French cooking and fusion cooking. Fusion cuisine is a blend of cooking styles and ingredients from various nations. In 1981 Puck published his first cookbook — *Modern French Cooking for the American Kitchen*.

In the twenty-first century, Puck operates about one hundred restaurants in the United States. He has written many cookbooks. People can also buy his packaged foods at grocery stores.

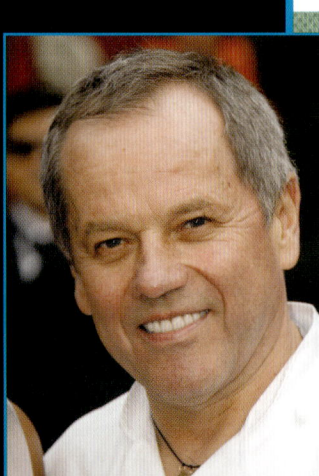

68 • THE EUROPEAN AMERICAN EXPERIENCE

Cajun crawfish boils are popular in Louisiana. Cooks boil the crawfish in large pots along with potatoes, corn on the cob, and sausage.

Cajun cooking includes many African, Spanish, and Caribbean influences, as well as local Louisiana ingredients such as fresh shrimp, crawfish, oysters, and crab. Cajun cuisine has many French ingredients as well, including boudin (French-style sausage) and roux (flour and butter or oil, used to thicken soups and sauces).

FAMOUS EUROPEAN AMERICANS

Antonio Banderas (b. 1960)

Antonio Banderas is a leading Hollywood actor. Growing up in Málaga, Spain, Banderas dreamed of becoming a professional soccer player. At the age of fourteen, he broke his foot. The injury forced him to choose a different career goal, so he turned to acting. Throughout the 1980s, he appeared in Spanish-made films. By his early thirties, Banderas was playing leading roles in Hollywood. In 1998 Banderas starred in *The Mask of Zorro*. The film is based on a series of books about a fictional masked Mexican swordsman. Banderas's other films include *Philadelphia* (1993) and *Evita* (1996). He also played the father in the *Spy Kids* movies and the voice of Puss in Boots in the *Shrek* film series.

Sergey Brin (b. 1973)

Brin, a Russian American, is cocreator of the Internet company Google. Brin was born in Moscow, Russia (in the former Soviet Union). His family moved to the United States when he was six years old to escape anti-Semitism, or discrimination against Jews. The Brins settled in Washington, D.C. There, for the first time in their lives, they were able to attend a synagogue and freely practice the Jewish faith. Sergey went to Hebrew school as well as public high school. He finished high school in three years instead of four. He attended the University of Maryland and Stanford University in California, where he studied computer science. He met Larry Page at Stanford. The two men created an Internet search engine. They named it Google, an intentional misspelling of the number googol (the number one followed by one hundred zeros).

Arianna Huffington (b. 1950)

Arianna Huffington (born Arianna Stassinopoulos) was born in Athens, Greece. She moved to Britain at the age of sixteen and graduated from Cambridge University with a degree in economics. After working for a time in London, she moved to the United States in 1980. Huffington has written eleven books on politics and the arts. She has also worked as a political commentator on numerous television and radio programs. In May 2005, Huffington founded the *Huffington Post*, a widely read news website. She is the site's editor in chief.

Milla Jovovich (b. 1975)

Jovovich is an actress and model born in Kiev, Ukraine (then part of the Soviet Union). Her Serbian father was a doctor. Her Russian mother was an actress. Her family left Ukraine in 1981. They settled in Los Angeles. In school Milla felt rejected by other students, who called her names because of her eastern European background. She turned to modeling at the age of eleven. She modeled for Revlon and later for Banana Republic, Christian Dior, the Gap, and L'Oréal. She soon attracted the attention of Hollywood directors. She played her first leading role in *Return to the Blue Lagoon* (1991). Since then she has appeared in dozens of films, including the *Resident Evil* series and *Zoolander* (2001).

John F. Kennedy (1917–1963)

Kennedy was the first Catholic and the youngest person ever to be elected president of the United States. He was the great-grandson of poor Irish immigrants who escaped the Great Famine. By the time John was born, however, the Kennedy family was wealthy. Growing up in Boston, John had a privileged childhood. He attended the best schools in Massachusetts and then New York. In 1936 he enrolled at Harvard University. He served as a commander in the U.S. Navy during World War II and won several medals for heroic acts. He started his political career in 1946 as a U.S. congressman from Massachusetts. In 1952 he won a U.S. Senate seat representing Massachusetts. In 1961, at the age of forty-three, Kennedy was elected the thirty-fifth president of the United States. An assassin killed Kennedy in November 1963.

Tara Lipinski (b. 1982)

Lipinski is a Polish American figure skater. She was born in Philadelphia, Pennsylvania, and raised in New Jersey, Texas, and Delaware. She began roller-skating at the age of three and turned to ice-skating at the age of six. In 1997, after extensive training, Lipinski won the U.S. and World Figure Skating Championships. She was fourteen years old at the time and the youngest person to win either title. The following year, at the 1998 Olympics, she won a gold medal in women's individual figure skating. In 1998 Lipinski published a book called *Totally Tara: An Olympic Journey*.

EXPLORE YOUR HERITAGE

Where did your family come from? Who are your relatives, and where do they live? Were they born in the United States? If not, when and why did they come here? Where did you get your family name? Is it German? Puerto Rican? Vietnamese? Something else? If you are adopted, what is your adoptive family's story?

By searching for the answers to these questions, you can begin to discover your family's history. And if your family history is hard to trace, team up with a friend to share ideas or to learn more about that person's family history.

Where to Start

Start with what you know. In a notebook or on your family's computer, write down the full names of the relatives you know about and anything you know about them—where they lived, what they liked to do as children, any awards or honors they earned, and so on.

Next, gather some primary sources. Primary sources are the records and observations of eyewitnesses to events. They include diaries; letters; autobiographies; speeches; newspapers; birth, marriage, and death records; photographs; and ship records. The best primary resources about your family may be in family scrapbooks or files in your home or in your relatives' homes. You may also find some interesting material in libraries, archives, historical societies, and museums. These organizations often have primary sources available online.

The Next Steps

After taking notes and gathering primary sources, think about what facts and details you are missing. You can then prepare to interview your relatives to see if they can fill in these gaps. First, write down any questions that you would like to ask them about their lives. Then ask your relatives if they would mind being interviewed. Don't be upset if they say no. Understand that some people do not like to talk about their pasts.

Also, consider interviewing family friends. They can often provide interesting stories and details about your relatives. They might have photographs too.

Family Interviews

When you are ready for an interview, gather your questions, a notepad, a tape recorder or camcorder, and any other materials you might need. Consider showing your interview subjects a photograph or a timetable of important events at the start of your interview. These items can help jog the memory of your subjects and get them talking. You might also bring U.S. and world maps to an interview. Ask your subjects to label the places they have lived.

Remember that people's memories aren't always accurate. Sometimes they forget information and confuse dates. You might want to take a trip to the library or look online to check dates and other facts.

Get Organized!

When you finish your interviews and research, you are ready to organize your information. There are many ways of doing this. You can write a history of your entire family or individual biographies of your relatives. You can create a timeline going back to your earliest known ancestors. You can make a family tree—a diagram or chart that shows how people in your family are related to one another.

If you have collected a lot of photographs, consider compiling a photo album or scrapbook that tells your family history. Or if you used a camcorder to record your interviews, you might even want to make a movie.

However you put together your family history, be sure to share it! Your relatives will want to see all the information you found. You might want to create a website or blog so that other people can learn about your family. Whatever you choose to do, you'll end up with something your family will appreciate for years to come.

EUROPEAN AMERICAN SNAPSHOT

This chart affords a statistical snapshot of five European American groups living in the United States. It looks at how many European Americans from each group are living in the country and which states have the greatest populations. All figures are based on individuals claiming full or partial ancestry in the 2000 U.S. Census.

	TOTAL U.S. POPULATION	FIVE TOP STATES OF RESIDENCE	YEARS OF GREATEST IMMIGRATION
German	42,885,162	California: 3,319,422 Pennsylvania: 3,119,388 Ohio: 2,860,991 Illinois: 2,434,181 Wisconsin: 2,306,380	1840–1900
Irish	30,594,130	California: 2,608,117 New York: 2,447,963 Pennsylvania: 1,977,250 Florida: 1,646,185 Texas: 1,501,331	1845–1880
English	24,515,138	California: 2,506,502 Florida: 1,470,379 New York: 1,138,587 Ohio: 1,044,489 Michigan: 983,906	1600s–1865
Italian	15,723,555	New York: 3,254,298 New Jersey: 1,590,225 Pennsylvania: 1,547,470 Massachusetts: 1,518,838 California: 1,149,351	1876–1924
Polish	8,977,235	New York: 986,141 Illinois: 932,996 Michigan: 854,844 Pennsylvania: 824,146 New Jersey: 576,473	1870–1914

GLOSSARY

accent: a distinctive way of pronouncing words common to a specific group or region

Americanize: to conform to U.S. culture and the characteristics of mainstream Americans

anti-Semitism: discrimination against Jews

colony: a group of people living in a new territory but maintaining ties to their home country

dialect: a regional variation on a language

discrimination: treating someone differently because of his or her ethnic background, race, religion, or gender

emigrate: to leave one's home country for another country

famine: a severe shortage of food

fluent: capable of using a language easily and accurately

immigrate: to enter a new country in order to live there

missionary: a religious teacher who tries to convert others to his or her faith

persecute: to harass or punish someone for his or her beliefs or background

SELECTED BIBLIOGRAPHY

Abramson, Edward A. "The Immigrant Experience in American Literature." British Association for American Studies, 1982. http://www.baas.ac.uk/resources/pamphlets/pamphdets.asp?id=10 (July 24, 2009).

Brittingham, Angela, and G. Patricia de la Cruz. "Ancestry: 2000, Census 2000 Brief," U.S. Census Bureau, June 2004. http://www.census.gov/prod/2004pubs/c2kbr-35.pdf (May 28, 2009).

Coffey, Michael, ed. *The Irish in America*. New York: Hyperion, 1997.

Daniels, Roger. *Coming to America: A History of Immigration and Ethnicity in American Life.* 2nd ed. New York: HarperCollins, 2002.

Dickie, John. *Delizia! The Epic History of the Italians and Their Food*. New York: Free Press, 2008.

Gottlieb, Jack. *Funny, It Doesn't Sound Jewish*. Albany: State University of New York, 2004.

Gould, Philip, and Barry Jean Ancelet. *Cajun Music and Zydeco*. Baton Rouge: Louisiana State University Press, 1992.

Guinta, Edvige. *Writing with an Accent: Contemporary Italian American Women Authors*. New York: Palgrave, 2002.

Lynn, Karyl. *The National Trust Guide to Great Opera Houses in America*. New York: John Wiley and Sons, 1996.

Tidwell, Mike. *Bayou Farewell: The Rich Life and Tragic Death of Louisiana's Cajun Coast*. New York: Pantheon Books, 2003.

FURTHER READING AND WEBSITES

Accents of English from around the World
http://www.soundcomparisons.com
Open this amazing website to hear recordings of English accents throughout the world—and back in time. Click on "North America" to hear different accents from the United States.

Anderson, Catherine Corley. *John F. Kennedy*. Minneapolis: Twenty-First Century Books, 2004.
This biography in the Presidential Leaders series details the professional and personal life of John F. Kennedy, along with important historical, political, and social issues of his time.

Bartoletti, Susan Campbell. *Black Potatoes: The Story of the Great Irish Famine, 1845–1850*. Boston: Houghton Mifflin, 2001.
The author uses eyewitness accounts and memories of Irish people to tell the story of the tragic famine in Ireland.

Behnke, Alison. *Italians in America*. Minneapolis: Lerner Publications Company, 2005.
This book examines life in Italy before emigration and the experiences of Italian Americans afterward.

Early "Actuality" Films
http://www.celluloidskyline.com/general/actualities.html
This website provides a collection of early films depicting life in New York in the late 1800s and early 1900s. The short clips portray real scenes, including European immigrants arriving at Ellis Island, a large immigration center in New York.

Easy Menu Ethnic Cookbooks series. Minneapolis: Lerner Publications Company, 2002–2005.
These easy-to-follow cookbooks weave together the history, culture, and cuisine of countries from around the world. To learn more about European cooking, readers can check out *Cooking the English Way, Cooking the French Way, Cooking the German Way, Cooking the Italian Way, Cooking the Mediterranean Way, Desserts around the World*, and *Holiday Cooking around the World*.

Goldstein, Margaret J. *British in America*. Minneapolis: Lerner Publications Company, 2006.
The British were the first Europeans to settle in North America, and their culture set the stage for much of U.S. culture. This book examines the British American experience.

Gundisch, Karin. *How I Became an American*. Peterborough, NH: Cricket Books, 2001.
In this fictional book, a family leaves Austria-Hungary for the United States in the early 1900s. Although the story is fiction, the author weaves in letters written by real immigrants.

Hasday, Judy L. *Americans of Eastern European Heritage*. Broomall, PA: Mason Crest Publishers, 2009.
From the Successful Americans series, this book looks at the lives of famous eastern European Americans.

USA Today Lifeline Biographies. Minneapolis: Twenty-First Century Books, 2009–2011.
Read profiles of Sergey Brin, Danica Patrick, and other prominent European Americans in this series.

INDEX

Amish, 13, 46
Andretti, Mario, 35, 36
Appalachia, 13, 26
art and architecture, 31–32
auto racing, 35, 36

Baltimore Basilica, 50–51
Banderas, Antonio, 70
baseball, 37, 38
basketball, 42, 43
BeauSoleil, 21
Bennett, Tony, 22
Bono, 16
Brando, Marlon, 28
Brin, Sergey, 70
British immigrants, 5, 16–17, 45
Bulgaria, 32, 49

Cagney, James, 28
Cajuns, 14, 21, 67, 69
Caruso, Enrico, 22
Cassini, Oleg, 33
Cather, Willa, 18
Catholicism, 45, 48–49, 50–51, 57
Child, Julia, 64, 65
Christianity, 46, 48–49, 52–54, 55, 56
Christo, 32
clogging, 26
Columbus Day, 58–59
cooking. *See* food
Cooper, James Fenimore, 14, 16
cycling, 39

dance, 24–27
Da Ponte, Lorenzo, 22
Declaration of Independence, 8
Denmark, 13, 68
DeSalvo, Louise, 19
Dietrich, Marlene, 27

Eastern Orthodoxy, 49
Ellis Island, 4, 5
England, 5, 8, 46, 67–68, 74
Europe, 9; reasons for emigration from, 5–6

fashion, 32–33
figure skating, 40
Finland, 13, 32, 68
flamenco, 26–27
food: ethnic food and restaurants, 61–63; fondue, 64, 67; French cooking, 64, 65; haute cuisine, 61; Mediterranean, 61, 67; most popular ethnic, 67; recipes, 63, 66; regional cooking, 67–69
football, 35
France, 11, 14, 15, 35, 48, 64

genealogy, 72–73
Germany, 11, 12, 13, 27, 37, 42, 46, 58, 63, 67, 74
golf, 37
Greece, 30, 35, 49, 62
gymnastics, 40

hockey, 37, 41
holidays, 55–59
Huffington, Arianna, 70

immigrants from Europe: adoption of words from, 11–14; countries of origin, 14, 74; hardships, 6; language and cultural differences, 6–7, 8–10; reasons for immigrating, 5–6; working conditions, 18–19
Ireland, 6, 12, 19, 28, 30, 35, 48, 57–58, 74
Islam, 47, 55
Italy, 11, 19, 21–24, 28–29, 35, 53–54, 58–59, 62, 67, 74

Jewish immigrants, 11, 20–21, 37, 49–51, 54, 62
Jovovich, Milla, 71

Judaism, 49–51, 54

Kennedy, Jacqueline, 33
Kennedy, John F., 71
King, Betsy, 37
klezmer music, 20–21

Lady Gaga, 24
language issues, 8–17
Latrobe, Henry, 50–51
Laurie, Hugh, 17
LeMond, Greg, 39
Lipinski, Tara, 40, 71
literature, 14–19
Lithuania, 48
Liukin, Nastia, 40
Lollobrigida, Gina, 32–33
Louisiana, 12, 14, 15, 21, 55, 56

Madonna, 16, 24
Mardi Gras, 55, 56
Martin, Dean, 22
McCourt, Frank, 19
Meola, Tony, 38–39
Moberg, Vilhelm, 17–18
movies, 27–30
music, 20–24

New Orleans, 55, 56
newspapers, 9
Norway, 13, 16–17, 46, 68
Nowitzki, Dirk, 42, 43

opera, 21
Ovechkin, Alex, 41

Patrick, Danica, 35
Penn, William, 45
Poland, 24, 37, 40, 48, 74
polka, 24, 25
Protestantism, 46
Puck, Wolfgang, 68

Puritans, 45, 53

Quakers, 45–46

Ramadan, 55
recipes: potato soup, 63; skewered lamb, 66
religion, 5, 45–52
Romania, 37, 40
Russia, 40, 49
Ruth, Babe, 37, 38

Saarinen, Eero, 32
Scandinavia, 13, 68
Schwarzenegger, Arnold, 17, 29
Scotland, 13, 20
Serbia, 49
Sheridan, Jim, 30
Shteyngart, Gary, 19
Sinatra, Frank, 22, 23
Sinclair, Upton, 18–19
soccer, 38–39
Spain, 26–27, 48
sports, 35–43
Sturr, Jimmy, 25
Sweden, 13, 17–18, 27, 46, 68
swimming, 40

tennis, 35
Theron, Charlize, 17
Thibodeaux, Waylon, 21
Turner, Tina, 16

Ukraine, 53

Vardalos, Nia, 30

Wall, Eamonn, 19
Weismuller, Johnny, 40

Yastrzemski, Carl, 37
Youkilis, Kevin, 37

PHOTO ACKNOWLEDGMENTS

The images in this book are used with the permission of: Library of Congress, p. 3 (top, LC-DIG-ggbain-30546), 4 (LC-DIG-ggbain-30546); © Hemis.fr/SuperStock, pp. 3 (second from top), 15; AP Photo/Mary Altaffer, pp. 3 (third from top), 20; © Pascal Rondeau/Allsport/Getty Images, pp. 3 (middle), 39 (bottom); © Dian Stevenson/USA TODAY, pp. 3 (third from bottom), 44; AP Photo/M. Spencer Green, pp. 3 (second from bottom), 57; © Coburn A. Dukehart/USA TODAY, pp. 3 (bottom), 69; © Image Asset Management Ltd./SuperStock, pp. 5, 6; National Archives, p. 8; © Felix Koch/Cincinnati Museum Center/Getty Images, p. 10; © SuperStock/SuperStock, pp. 12, 71 (top); © Eileen Blass/USA TODAY, pp. 13, 71 (bottom); © New York Times Co./Archive Photos/Getty Images, p. 18; © Ulf Andersen/Getty Images, p. 19; AP Photo/Bill Haber, p. 21; AP Photo, pp. 22, 65; © Herbert Gehr/Time & Life Pictures/Getty Images, p. 23; © Dimitrios Kambouris/WireImage for Marc Jacobs/Getty Images, p. 24; © Ebet Roberts/Redferns/Getty Images, p. 25; AP Photo/The Holland Sentinel, Dan Irving, p. 26; © Gjon Mili/Time & Life Pictures/Getty Images, p. 27 (top); © Evening Standard/Hulton Archive/Getty Images, p. 27 (bottom); Paramount/The Kobal Collection, p. 28; © Tim Dillon/USA TODAY, p. 29; IFC Films/The Kobal Collection/Giraud, Sophie, p. 30; AP Photo/Adam Rountree, p. 31; © Michael Madrid/USA TODAY, p. 32; AP Photo/Remo Nassi, p. 33 (top); © Leonard McCombe/Time & Life Pictures/Getty Images, p. 33 (bottom); © Robert Deutsch/USA TODAY, p. 34; © AJ Mast/USA TODAY, p. 35; AP Photo/Michael Conroy, p. 36; © Al Messerschmidt/WireImage/Getty Images, p. 37; AP Photo/National Baseball Library, Cooperstown, N.Y., p. 38; © Ed Zurga/MLS/Allsport/Getty Images, p. 39 (top); © Jessica Rinaldi/USA TODAY, p. 40; © Emile Wamsteker/USA TODAY, p. 41 (bottom); © Robert Hanashiro/USA TODAY, pp. 42, 70 (bottom); © Stock Montage/SuperStock, p. 45; © James Nubile/The Image Works, p. 47; © age fotostock/SuperStock, pp. 49, 54; AP Photo/Matt Houston, p. 51; © IndexStock/SuperStock, p. 52; AP Photo/Alex Brandon, p. 56; © Steve Kelley/Flickr/Getty Images, p. 59; © Jupiterimages/Comstock Images/Getty Images, p. 60; © Craig Mitchelldyer/USA TODAY, p. 61; AP Photo/Jose F. Moreno, p. 62; © Luna/StockFood Creative/Getty Images, p. 64; © Dan MacMedan/USA TODAY, p. 68; © Todd Plitt/USA TODAY, p. 70 (top); ©Stephen Higgins/USA TODAY, p. 70 (middle); AP Photo/Tammie Arroyo, p. 71 (middle); © Todd Strand/Independent Picture Service, pp. 72–73.

Front cover: AP Photo/M. Spencer Green (top); © Patti McConville/Photographer's Choice/Getty Images (bottom left); © age fotostock/SuperStock (bottom right).

ABOUT THE AUTHOR

Karen Sirvaitis is a freelance writer and editor. She has written more than twenty books. She lives in northwestern Wisconsin with her family.

973.04 S   ICCRX
Sirvaitis, Karen,
The European American experience /

CENTRAL LIBRARY
07/11